LET'S BUILD A HOUSE

A White Cottage before Winter

Written and Illustrated by
Russ Flint

IDEALS CHILDREN'S BOOKS
Nashville, Tennessee

Published by Ideals Publishing Corporation
Nashville, Tennessee 37214

Printed and bound in the United States of America.

Library of Congress Cataloging-in-Publication Data

Flint, Russ.
Let's build a house: a white cottage before winter / written
and illustrated by Russ Flint.
p.cm.
Summary: Identifies and explains the materials and steps
involved in building a house from foundation to rooftop.
ISBN 0-8249-8432-3
1. House construction—Juvenile literature.
[1. House construction.]   I. Title.
TH4811.5.F59   1990
690'.837—dc20   89-29425
                                                 CIP
                                                 AC

For Beth, Rusty, Rod,
and
Dorinda

- R. F.

My name is Dorinda and I'm sitting on my dad's shoulders.

We usually have picnics here—it's my favorite place. Now we want to buy this land and build a new house here! We would like to get started right away, but there is much to be done before the first nail can be hammered.

First we have to find out if there is plenty of fresh water for bathing, washing, and drinking. If fresh water can be found underground, we will buy the land and start building our new house.

We will have to hurry because winter is almost here.

A well driller was hired to look for fresh water underground. First, he looks for clues that show him where to find water. Certain plants grow where there is underground water.

Once he has found the right place, he backs his truck into position and drills a hole deep into the ground. When his drill hits sand and gravel, he knows that water is nearby.

He's found water, so now we can buy the land and start building our house.

Workers will drop pipes into the well driller's hole, fasten them together, and pour wet concrete around them. This will be our well.

We will put an electric pump in the water at the bottom of the well. The pump will push water up through the pipes and into the house whenever we need it.

The ground must be smooth and flat to build on, so the bulldozer is clearing and leveling a space for the house.

My dad cut down the old, dead oak tree because a wind storm could have easily blown it against the house. The tree stump—and any dead wood—must be taken away because it invites termites and termites eat wood.

The man on the power pole is a worker from the electric company. He is hooking up the wires which will provide electricity for the electric tools needed to build the house.

The backhoe is digging a trench in the shape of the bottom of our house. The backhoe also dug a big hole where my brothers are standing. This hole is for the septic tank.

Just as there is no city water to pipe into the house, there is also no sewer to take the wastewater away from the house. Wastewater will be piped from the house and into the septic tank. The tank should be delivered today.

A truck from the lumber company delivered all the lumber we will need to build the house. Dad and Grandpa used some of this lumber to build the wooden form around the trench.

Wet concrete oozes out of the cement truck down the long chute into the wooden form as a worker guides it with a piece of plywood.

Dad pokes at the concrete with a pole to get rid of air pockets which weaken the concrete. And Grandpa smooths the top of the concrete so that it will be flat when it dries.

When the concrete is almost dry, the wooden forms will be taken away, leaving short, square walls above the ground. These walls are called the foundation.

After the concrete foundation is dry, boards are laid flat and bolted around the top of the foundation. This is called the mud sill.

The long boards set in a row on their sides are called floor joists. My brother Rod is walking on one of these joists.

Mom and Rod are laying blankets of insulation between the joists to help keep the floor warm in the winter and cool in the summer. Dad and Grandpa are nailing down the floorboards to the joists as Jeremy cuts each board to size.

With the floorboards in place, it is time to begin building the walls. First they must be framed. Framing provides a skeleton to support the house. Materials for framing the walls are laid out flat and nailed together. They are then lifted into place.

My dog Shorty is standing between the tall boards called studs. The board under his front paws is called the bottom plate. He is looking at a squirrel on the top plate.

The rectangular openings around the bottom of the house are called vents. The vents allow air to circulate under the house.

When a house has upstairs rooms, these rooms are called the second story. Jeremy and Dad are nailing down the floor boards for the second story.

Thick boards called headers are positioned over each doorway and window to provide extra strength above these openings.

Grandpa is nailing sheets of plywood to each corner of the house. Plywood will be added to the rest of the walls after the electrical wiring is strung through the studs. The plywood provides shear strength which makes the house strong.

Once the flooring for the second story is complete, the frame for the rest of the house can be built. The two walls which come to a point at the top are called gable walls. The long board that runs between the points of the two gable walls is called a ridge beam.

Meanwhile, my brothers are mixing concrete for the wellhouse foundation. Dry cement and sand are shoveled into the mixer to be mixed with water. Rod is bringing salt water from the ocean, but it can't be used because salt would make the concrete crumble when it dried.

Grandpa will pour the wet concrete into the small, square form near the well pipe. This will be the foundation of the wellhouse.

We can now see the shape of the roof. The slanted boards, called rafters, are attached to both the ridge beam and the top of the outside walls.

Dad is drilling holes in the wall studs. He will string electrical wire through these holes to bring electricity into the house.

Meanwhile, the wellhouse has been framed. Fresh water is pumped through the white pipes into the house. The black pipes will take the wastewater from the house to the septic tank.

The man getting out of his car is the building inspector. His job is to make sure that everything is being built the right way.

After Dad finished the wiring, ply-wood was nailed to the sides of the house. Dad is now nailing sheets of plywood to the rafters. This is called decking.

On the other end of the roof, Jeremy is tacking overlapping rolls of roofing felt to the decking. Roofing felt contains an oil which leaks out as the sun warms the roof. This oil seals the nail holes in the decking.

Outside the side door, a form has been built to hold wet concrete for making steps like those at the front door. The wooden form will be taken away before the concrete is dry.

Jeremy is finishing the roof. He slips each wooden shingle halfway under the roofing felt and nails it into place. He overlaps each shingle so that water will run off the roof when it rains. This keeps water from leaking into the house.

Masons are people who work with concrete and brick. They are building the chimney by arranging bricks in layers with wet concrete between each one to hold the bricks together.

The windows were assembled and ready to be put into place when they were delivered. The window on the second floor with its own little roof is called a dormer window.

The truck with our septic tank is finally here—it should have been delivered a long time ago! The truck lowers the septic tank into the hole in the ground.

While Dad and Grandpa are working on the outside, Mom and Grandma are working inside. The electrical wiring has already been strung through the holes in the studs. Now Mom and Grandma staple strips of insulation between the wall studs. Like the insulation under the flooring, this will help keep the house cooler in the summer and warmer in the winter.

Once the insulation is in place, workers hang sheets of drywall. Each sheet is tacked into place with nails at each corner. Later, screws will be used to secure each sheet permanently.

One man is using a long tool called a bazooka which fills each joint between the sheets of drywall with wet plaster and covers it with tape. After the walls have been painted, they will look smooth—none of the joints between the sheets will show.

Sometimes changes are made while a house is being built. At first, Mom wanted the house to be painted white. But since the house is surrounded by white sand, she has decided that it should be painted red.

The painters are standing on scaffolding, which fits together in sections so that it can be made either taller or shorter, or even moved to a different place.

They are using a spray gun to paint the house. The machine on the ground pushes air and paint through a hose and into the spray gun.

The temporary power pole has been disconnected because electrical power now runs directly into the house.

Jeremy and Grandpa are nailing the last of the board siding to the house.

The two small pipes on the roof are vent pipes. They provide air for the water pipes so that water will keep flowing when it is turned on.

Even though the house is ready for us to move into now, there are still things left to do. Dad says we will need to put a wind deflector on the top of the chimney so that the smoke won't blow so close to the top of the house. Mom says we have to figure out a way to get rid of all these puddles. And we want to build a white picket fence and plant rose bushes in the spring.

But the house is finished just in time for winter! I will live in my favorite place and this will be our home.

The St. Mary's Design by Preston Scheffenacker,
from The History Influenced House Collections of
Princeton Plans Press
Box 22, Princeton, NJ 08540

Technical advisors:
David Covington, Michael Banchio,
and Tyler Nichols